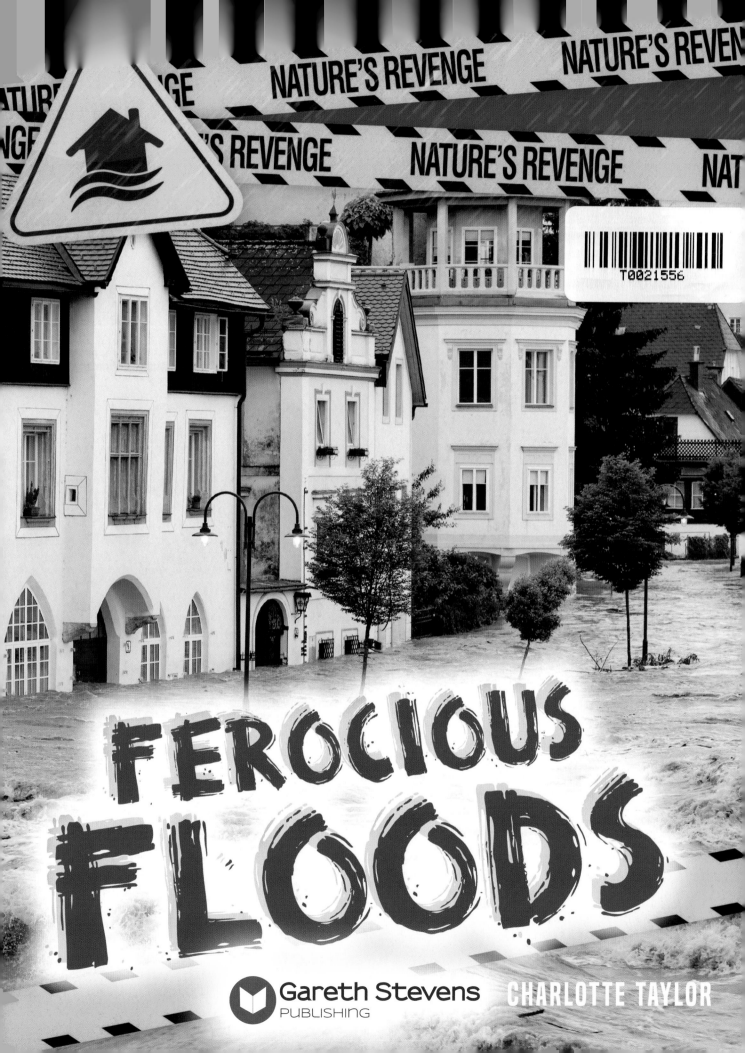

NATURE'S REVENGE

FEROCIOUS FLOODS

Gareth Stevens
PUBLISHING

CHARLOTTE TAYLOR

Please visit our website, www.garethstevens.com. For a free color catalog of all our high-quality books, call toll free 1-800-542-2595 or fax 1-877-542-2596.

Cataloging-in-Publication Data
Names: Taylor, Charlotte, 1978-.
Title: Ferocious floods / Charlotte Taylor.
Description: New York : Gareth Stevens Publishing, 2023. | Series: Nature's revenge | Includes glossary and index.
Identifiers: ISBN 9781538280638 (pbk.) | ISBN 9781538280652 (library bound) | ISBN 9781538280645 (6pack) | ISBN 9781538280669 (ebook)
Subjects: LCSH: Floods–Juvenile literature. | Natural disasters–Juvenile literature.
Classification: LCC GB1399.T39 2023 | DDC 363.34'93–dc23

Portions of this work were originally authored by Charles Hofer and published as *Washed Away by Floods*. All new material in this edition was authored by Charlotte Taylor.

Published in 2023 by
Gareth Stevens Publishing
29 East 21st Street
New York, NY 10010

Designer: Leslie Taylor
Editor: Megan Quick

Photo credits: Cover (flooded street) Lisa-S/Shutterstock.com; pp. 1–32 (icons-series artwork) Vector by/ Shutterstock.com; pp. 1–32 (hazard tape-series artwork) DDevecee/Shutterstock.com; p. 5 Matt Rourke, Associated Press/APImages.com; p. 7 VectorMine/Shutterstock.com; p. 9 Jason Lee, Associated Press/ APImages.com; p. 11 Melissa Phillip, Associated Press/APImages.com; p. 13 Andre Penner, Associated Press/APImages.com; p. 15 Anthony Behar, Sipa USA via AP/APImages.com; p. 17 Kevork Djansezian, Associated Press/APImages.com; p. 19 Liu Junfeng/APImages.com; p. 20 Keith Mecklem/Shutterstock. com; p. 21 https://commons.wikimedia.org/wiki/File:Oosterscheldekering,_Netherlands.JPG; p. 23 Jason Hoekema, Associated Press/APImages.com; p. 25 michelmond/Shutterstock.com; p. 27 trgrowth/ Shutterstock.com; p. 29 M. Volk/Shutterstock.com.

Printed in the United States of America

Some of the images in this book illustrate individuals who are models. The depictions do not imply actual situations or events.

CPSIA compliance information: Batch #CSGS23: For further information contact Gareth Stevens, New York, New York at 1-800-542-2595.

Find us on

CONTENTS

Wild Waters 4

Water on the Move 6

How a Flood Starts 8

Coastal Flooding 10

Overflowing Rivers 12

Flash Floods 14

Lasting Effects 16

Controlling Water's Power 18

Flood on the Way 22

Staying Safe 24

Earth Heats Up 26

Floods in the Future 28

Glossary 30

For More Information 31

Index 32

Words in the glossary appear in **bold** type the first time they are used in the text.

WILD WATERS

Floods are some of the most **dangerous** weather events in the world. They are also the most common type of natural **disaster**. Floods can come from streams, rivers, lakes, or oceans. They can knock out power, spread illness, and destroy homes. They are also deadly: Every year, people drown in floodwaters.

In some areas, flooding is becoming more common. Many scientists believe this is because of the world's changing **climate**. Our planet is slowly getting warmer, and it is causing lots of problems. One of those problems is **extreme** weather, like heavy rainfall and storms. This could mean we are in for more dangerous flooding if the planet continues to heat up.

This neighborhood in Philadelphia, Pennsylvania, was flooded after the city was soaked with heavy rains from the remains of Hurricane Ida in 2021.

Nature Unleashed

A flood is a type of natural disaster. This is an event in nature that causes a great deal of **damage**. Natural disasters can destroy buildings and hurt or kill people and animals. Besides floods, natural disasters include **hurricanes**, blizzards, and **earthquakes**.

WATER ON THE MOVE

About two-thirds of Earth is covered in water. That water is found in oceans, snow, ice, and underground in layers of rock or sand. It is all part of Earth's water supply, which moves between the land, oceans, and atmosphere, or the gases that surround Earth. This movement of water is called the water cycle.

Water in oceans, lakes, and rivers **evaporates** as it is warmed by the sun. It rises into the air as water vapor. As it gets higher in the atmosphere, it cools and becomes a liquid again. This is called condensation. The water gathers in clouds and falls back to Earth as rain or snow. Then the process starts all over again.

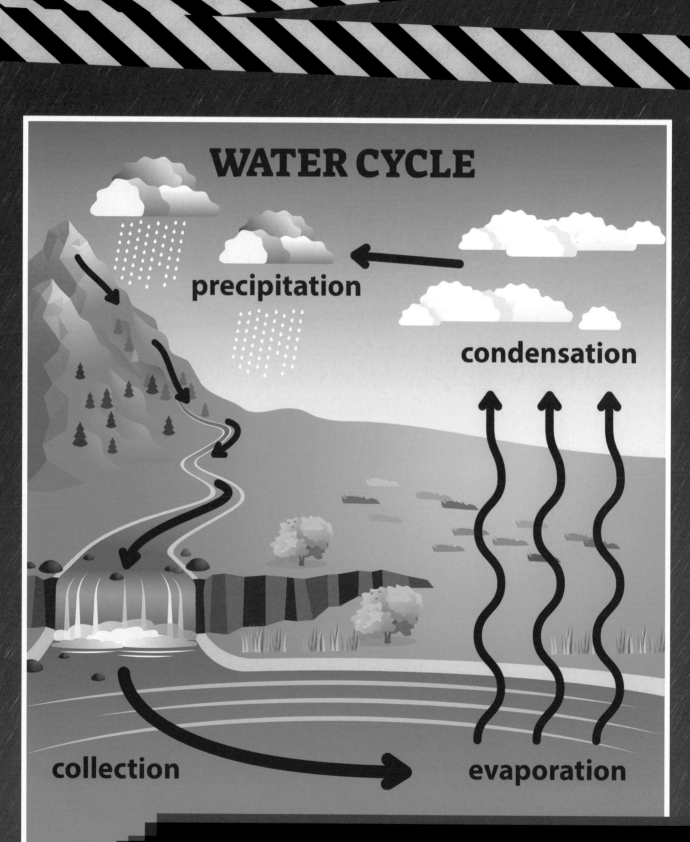

WATER CYCLE

precipitation

condensation

collection

evaporation

The water cycle is important because it brings water to all living things and allows us to have regular weather patterns.

HOW A FLOOD STARTS

Normally, rain or snow falls into a body of water or is **absorbed** into the ground. But events like heavy rainfall can overload these areas. Rivers or lakes may overflow onto the surrounding ground, known as the floodplain. The ground may become too full of water. When the land can't absorb all of the water, it pools on the surface. This can lead to flooding.

Human-made surfaces such as paved roads contribute to floods too. Water can collect on them and build into a flood. A lack of plant life can also lead to flooding. The roots of grasses and trees in the soil soak up water. Without plants, water may flow over the land and collect somewhere else as a flood.

This river in South Carolina overflowed after almost 3 feet (0.9 m) of rain fell from a hurricane in 2018.

The Benefits of Floods

Huge floods can be very harmful, but smaller floods can be good for the land. Floods leave sand and other materials on the floodplain. This material contains minerals, which make the soil better for growing plants. Floods are also helpful because they can wash away harmful **chemicals** in the soil.

COASTAL FLOODING

Flooding often happens along the coast. The coast is the area where the land meets the sea, and it's often very large and flat. This makes it an ideal place for flooding. Some weather events, such as hurricanes, can cause a storm surge. A storm surge happens when seawater is pushed onto the coastal floodplain by strong winds. This can cause major flooding.

One of the worst floods in U.S. history was caused by coastal flooding in New Orleans, Louisiana. In August 2005, Hurricane Katrina pounded the city for days. The storm surge from the hurricane, along with very heavy rains, flooded the city. The huge amount of water along the coast rushed right over the seawalls and other structures meant to hold back floodwaters.

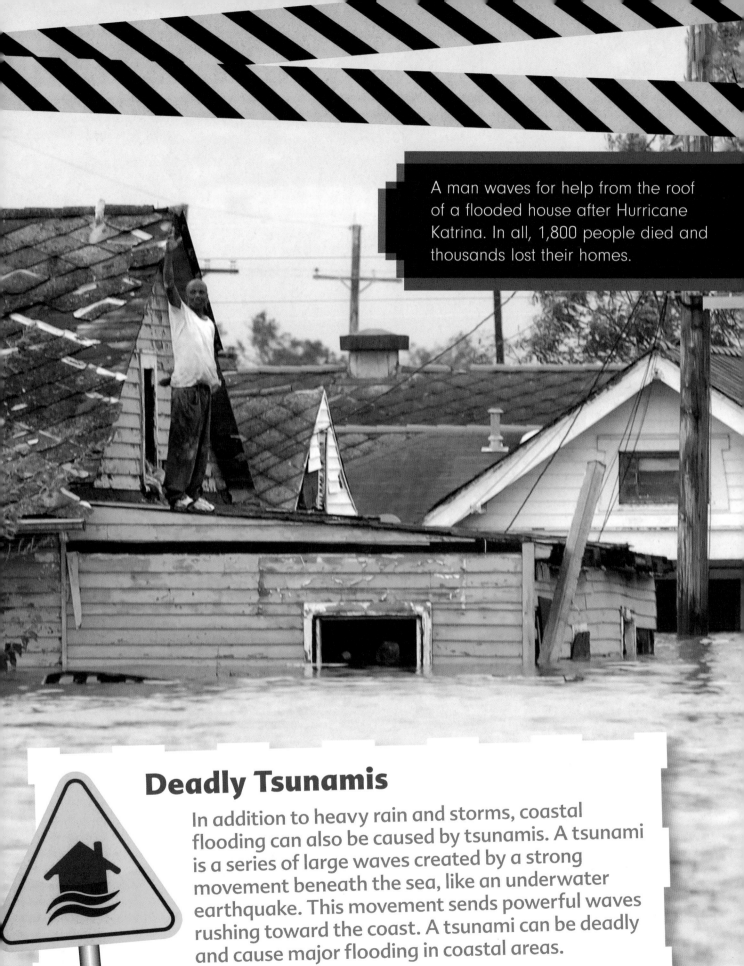

A man waves for help from the roof of a flooded house after Hurricane Katrina. In all, 1,800 people died and thousands lost their homes.

Deadly Tsunamis

In addition to heavy rain and storms, coastal flooding can also be caused by tsunamis. A tsunami is a series of large waves created by a strong movement beneath the sea, like an underwater earthquake. This movement sends powerful waves rushing toward the coast. A tsunami can be deadly and cause major flooding in coastal areas.

OVERFLOWING RIVERS

A river is part of a larger system of water. A small body of water, like a stream, feeds into a larger body of water, such as a river. That river might feed into a larger river or lake. Major rain events create problems when one part of the system is overloaded. The rivers and streams can overflow, sometimes causing serious flooding.

Snow and ice may also cause river flooding. Melting snow can add to the water levels in the river. Ice jams happen when ice blocks the river and causes water to build up behind ice. That water can end up spilling over onto the nearby land.

Heavy rains caused the Tietê and Pinheiros rivers in São Paulo, Brazil, to overflow and flood city streets in 2020.

At Home on the River

In America's early days, people often built towns near rivers. Living near a river provided an easy way to get water for drinking and farming. Rivers were also great for getting around, since boats could carry both people and goods. But with large populations living near water, floods could bring great danger to many people.

FLASH FLOODS

A flash flood is the deadliest kind of flood. It can happen when heavy rainfall causes water to build up very quickly. When the ground cannot absorb such a large amount of water, a sudden flood occurs. Flash floods can happen within hours or even minutes of heavy rain. They are very dangerous because there is little time to warn people of the risk.

Heavy rainfall is not the only cause of flash floods. A dam is a large structure that holds back water. If a dam breaks, the sudden burst of rushing water can flood any areas below it. An ice jam breaking and releasing built-up water can also result in a flash flood.

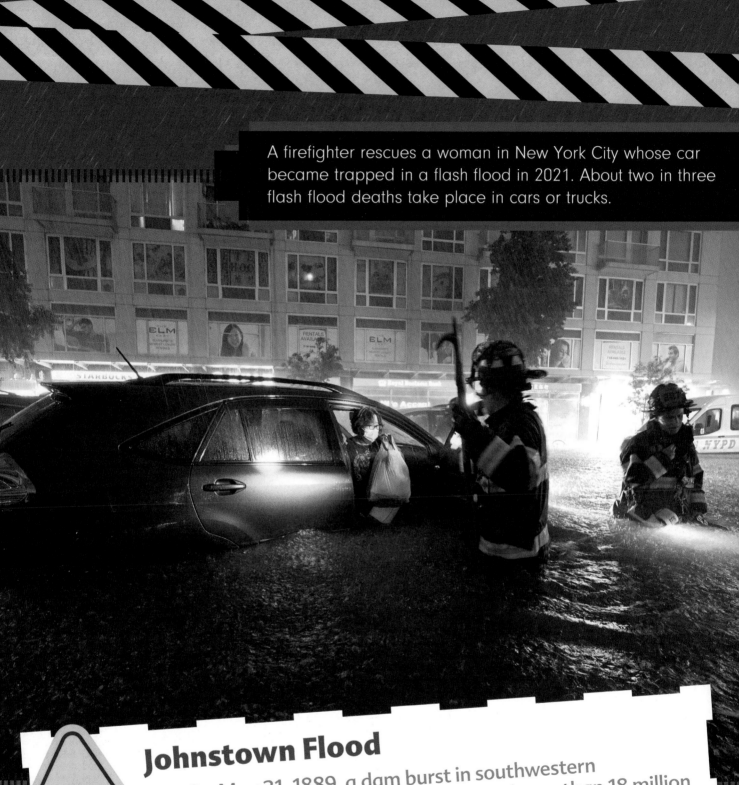

A firefighter rescues a woman in New York City whose car became trapped in a flash flood in 2021. About two in three flash flood deaths take place in cars or trucks.

Johnstown Flood

On May 31, 1889, a dam burst in southwestern Pennsylvania. About 20 million tons (more than 18 million metric tons) of water rushed downstream and slammed into the town of Johnstown. The wall of water was more than 30 feet (9 m) high and caused a giant flash flood. More than 2,200 people were killed and the town was wiped out. It was one of the worst floods in U.S. history.

LASTING EFFECTS

Floods can be harmful to people and property as well as the food and water supply. Water damage to homes and businesses can be difficult and expensive to fix. Floods can ruin crops. Dirty floodwaters can pollute fresh water supplies. Without enough food and water, flood survivors face new dangers.

Floodwaters can also take a long time to go away. Sometimes these waters can cause sickness. Standing water can attract mosquitoes, which are known to carry deadly illnesses such as malaria. **Mold** is another problem people face after floods. Deadly toxic mold grows in dark, damp places and may be present after floodwaters have gone.

A man stands in his New Orleans home after Hurricane Katrina. Mold, which is very unhealthy and expensive to remove, has spread over the walls and ceiling.

What's In the Water?

Floodwaters can hide many dangers, so it's important to stay out of them if possible. Downed power lines can cause harmful electricity in the water. Wildlife such as snakes and rats may be just under the surface. In a rare case in Louisiana, a man was attacked and killed by an alligator in floodwaters caused by Hurricane Ida in 2021.

CONTROLLING WATER'S POWER

It is impossible to control how much rain falls. However, it is possible to build structures that control the water once it reaches the ground. Dams hold back the flow of river water, while reservoirs are human-made lakes that collect the blocked water behind the dam. When too much water collects in the reservoir, it can be released through the dam in a controlled manner. This system can also provide water for drinking, for growing crops, or swimming.

Canals are used to reroute the flow of water. These long, human-made channels are lined with concrete or another hard material. Canals move extra water from one place to another, which greatly reduces the chance of flooding.

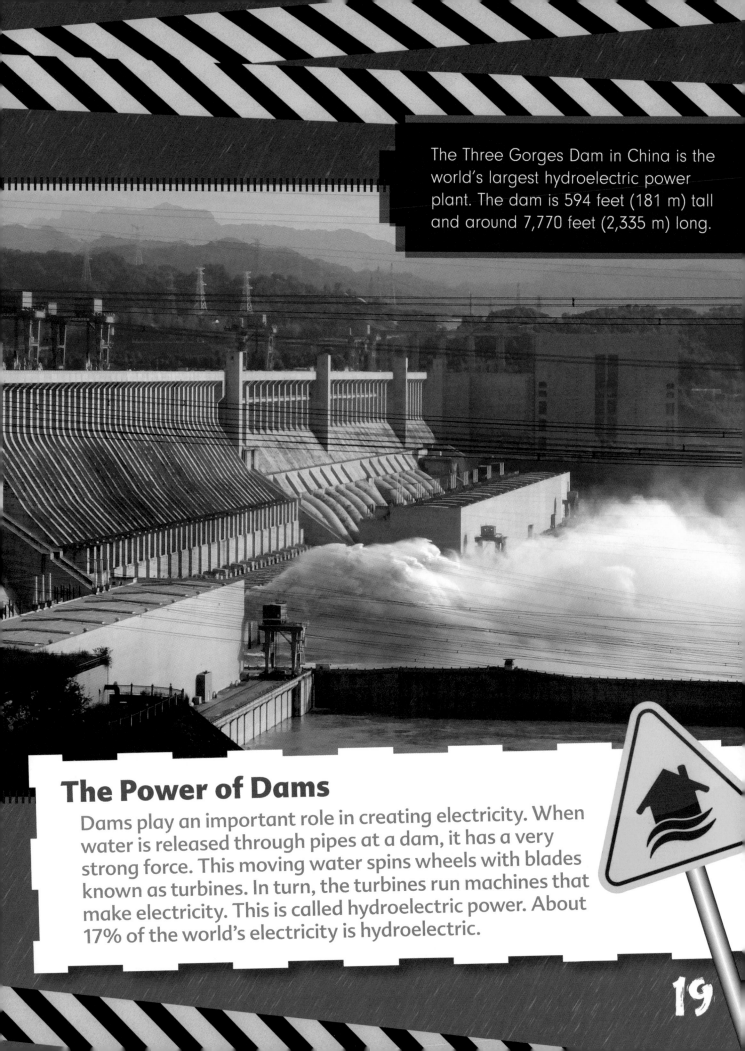

The Three Gorges Dam in China is the world's largest hydroelectric power plant. The dam is 594 feet (181 m) tall and around 7,770 feet (2,335 m) long.

The Power of Dams

Dams play an important role in creating electricity. When water is released through pipes at a dam, it has a very strong force. This moving water spins wheels with blades known as turbines. In turn, the turbines run machines that make electricity. This is called hydroelectric power. About 17% of the world's electricity is hydroelectric.

Floodwalls, also called levees, are another type of structure that protects against rising waters in times of flooding. These large walls or raised areas keep communities safe from flooding while sending extra water toward safer areas. Many cities and towns along the Mississippi River and other major waterways use floodwalls as part of their flood-control system.

Floods are a problem around the world. In the Netherlands, for example, more than half the country's residents live in areas below sea level. For that reason, the country has built a series of dams, canals, and other means to protect the land from storm surges. They've even created huge movable gates that can be closed to block out incoming seawater.

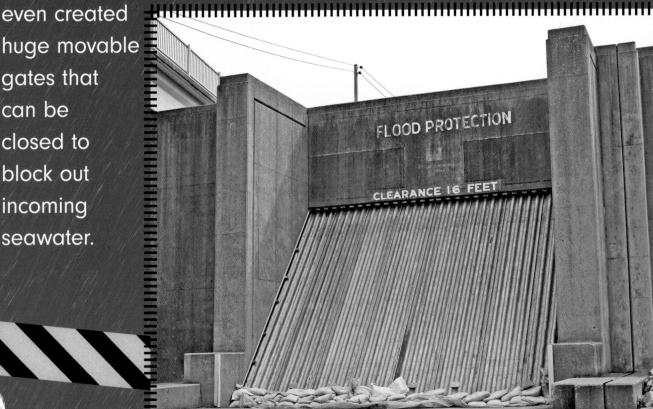

FLOOD PROTECTION

CLEARANCE 16 FEET

Disaster in Mississippi

Levees are helpful tools for preventing flooding, but they don't always work. In 1927, months of heavy rains caused the whole levee system along the Mississippi River to break down. Some areas were flooded with 30 feet (9 m) of water. About 250 people were killed and 600,000 lost their homes.

This human-made seawall is part of a large flood-control system in the Netherlands.

FLOOD ON THE WAY

How do we know if a flood might be on the way? Meteorologists are scientists who study weather, climate, and the atmosphere. They look at the amount and type of rainfall, the levels of the rivers, and the conditions of the ground. If they believe a flood might be coming, an **alert** goes out.

The National Weather Service issues alerts when severe weather is possible. The first stage of the flood alert system is an advisory. This tells people to be aware of possible flooding in their area. The second stage is a watch. This means conditions are right for flooding and severe floods are possible. The final stage is a warning. People should take action because a flood is occurring or is about to occur.

A meteorolgist uses computers to check possible rainfall amounts.

Emergency!

If meteorologists predict extreme flooding, such as the kind that comes with a hurricane, a state of emergency may be declared. This can be done on a state or national level. Once this happens, money and other types of help are made available to areas in need. They help to prepare for the severe weather and assist with any rescue, shelter, or cleanup needs.

STAYING SAFE

The best time to prepare for a flood is well before it happens. Keep an emergency kit with food, clean drinking water, and supplies such as a flashlight, first-aid kit, battery-powered radio, and extra batteries. Know your **evacuation** route and the location of the nearest emergency shelter.

Once a flood occurs, use the internet or radio to get the latest reports on conditions. Stay away from places such as basements, valleys, and other low-lying areas where flooding often occurs. Do not drive or walk through flooded areas. If you have to evacuate, don't return to your home after a flood until officials tell you it's safe to do so.

Families in Houston, Texas, check in at a shelter after Hurricane Harvey flooded the area in 2017. Many cities and towns set up emergency shelters after a natural disaster.

Car Smarts

Be careful if you are in a car near a flooded area. Even if the water does not look very deep, do not try to drive through a flooded road. It only takes 1 foot (0.3 m) of water to sweep a car away. If you find yourself in a car in rising waters, leave the car and find higher ground.

EARTH HEATS UP

Our planet is getting hotter. This is called global warming, and many scientists believe it is tied to extreme weather. Things we do every day contribute to global warming. When we drive, cook, or heat our homes, we often use **fossil fuels** like coal and oil. These fuels send gases into the air. The gases trap the sun's heat. Over time, Earth gets warmer.

As the world heats up, so do the oceans. This warm water evaporates and rises into the atmosphere, which means more water vapor in the air. This can lead to heavier rain and snow, which increases the chance for flooding.

Droughts and Floods

A drought is a long period of very dry weather. Floods and droughts have a lot in common. They are both very harmful and they are both made worse by global warming. More water evaporating into the atmosphere can leave land very dry. Dry land cannot absorb water quickly. Heavy rains that follow a drought can cause major flooding.

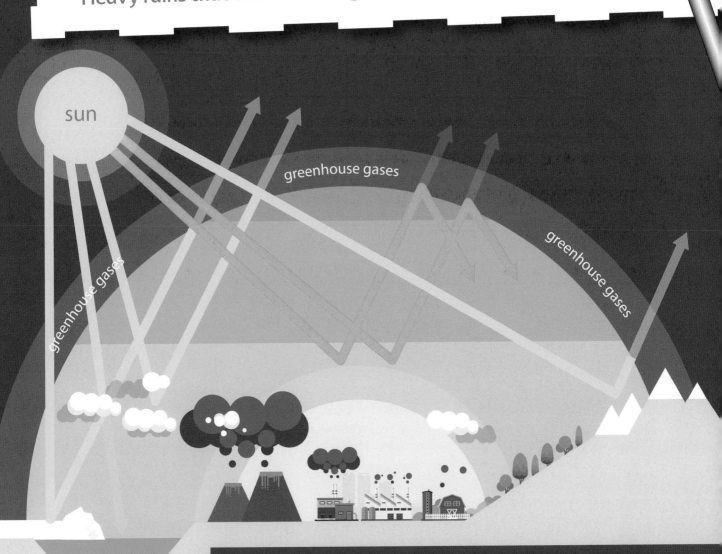

sun

greenhouse gases

greenhouse gases

greenhouse gases

Greenhouse gases, such as water vapor and carbon dioxide, are released into the atmosphere. The gases allow the sun's light to leave the atmosphere, but they trap the heat.

FLOODS IN THE FUTURE

If Earth's climate continues to change, it is likely that heavy flooding will become more common in many areas. But there are simple things that you can do to slow down global warming. Turn off lights when you leave a room. Shut down your computer when you're not using it. Walk or ride a bike instead of driving.

It will take a big effort by many people to control climate change. In the meantime, dangerous weather events like flooding are a fact of life. It's important to be aware of the risks and to plan ahead. Being prepared can help keep you and your family safe.

Save the Trees

Cutting down too many trees is a key cause of climate change. Trees keep Earth healthy by removing harmful gases from the atmosphere. Trees near bodies of water also help prevent flooding. If you want to help save the planet, save a tree! Use less paper, recycle, or plant a new tree.

The village of Monreal, Germany, flooded in 2021. As global warming continues, dangerous floods like this one may happen more often around the world.

GLOSSARY

absorb: to take in

alert: a warning

chemical: matter that can be mixed with other matter to cause changes

climate: the average weather conditions of a place over a period of time

damage: harm

dangerous: unsafe

disaster: an event that causes much suffering or loss

earthquake: a shaking of the ground caused by the movement of Earth's crust

evacuation: the act of leaving an area because of danger

evaporate: to change from a liquid to a gas

extreme: great or severe

fossil fuel: matter formed over millions of years from plant and animal remains that is burned for power

hurricane: a powerful storm that forms over water and causes heavy rainfall and high winds

mold: a soft substance that grows on the surface of damp or rotting things

FOR MORE INFORMATION

BOOKS

Drimmer, Stephanie. *National Geographic Kids Ultimate Weatherpedia.* Washington, DC: National Geographic Kids, 2019.

Dykstra, Mary. *Climate Change and Extreme Storms.* Minneapolis, MN: Lerner, 2019.

Haney, Johannah. *Natural Disasters!* Norwich, VT: Nomad Press, 2020.

WEBSITES

National Geographic Kids: What Is Climate Change?
www.natgeokids.com/uk/discover/geography/general-geography/what-is-climate-change/
Find out all about the causes and effects of climate change and how you can help.

NOAA SciJinks: Water and Ice
scijinks.gov/menu/water-and-ice/
Check out cool facts about floods and other kinds of precipitation.

Weather Wiz Kids: Rain and Floods
www.weatherwizkids.com/weather-rain.htm
Learn more about floods and try out some fun experiments with rain.

INDEX

advisory 22

canal 18, 20

dam 14, 15, 18, 19, 20

drought 27

floodplain 8, 9, 10

floodwall 20

global warming 26, 27, 28

greenhouse gases 27

Hurricane Harvey 25

Hurricane Ida 5, 17

Hurricane Katrina 10, 11, 17

hydroelectric power 19

ice jam 12, 14

Johnstown Flood 15

levee 20, 21

meteorologist 22, 23

National Weather Service 22

reservoir 18

storm surge 10, 20

Three Gorges Dam 19

tsunami 11

warning 22

watch 22

water cycle 6, 7

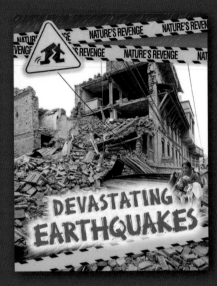

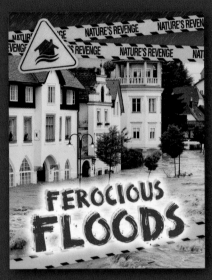

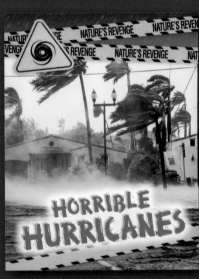

Gareth Stevens
PUBLISHING

ISBN: 9781538280638
6-pack ISBN: 9781538280645

9 781538 280638

NATURE'S REVENGE

TERRIBLE TSUNAMIS

CHARLOTTE TAYLOR